Shapes Everywhere

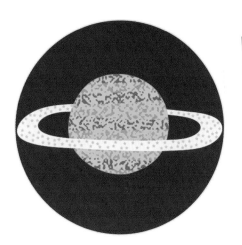

Written by Charlotte Raby

Illustrated by Sue Downing

Collins

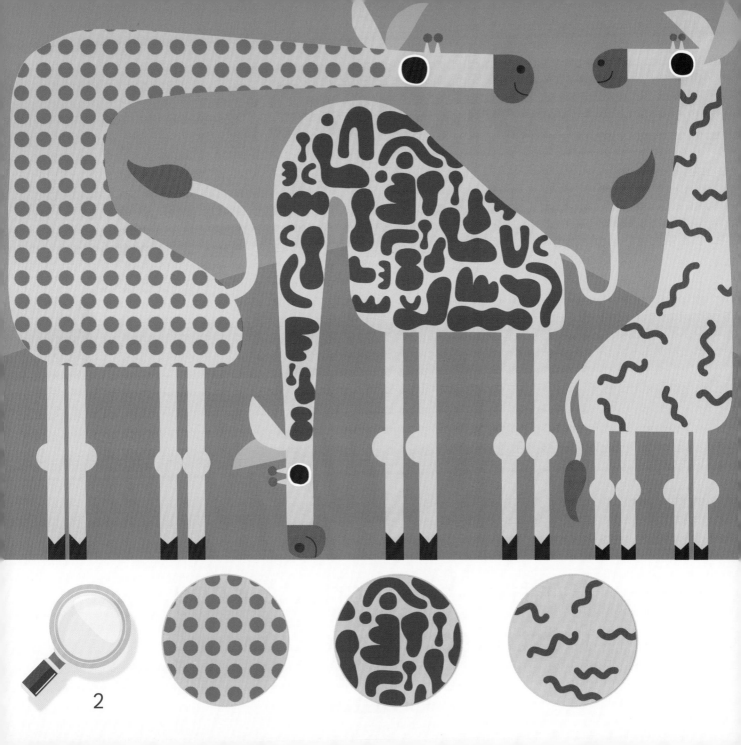

2

3

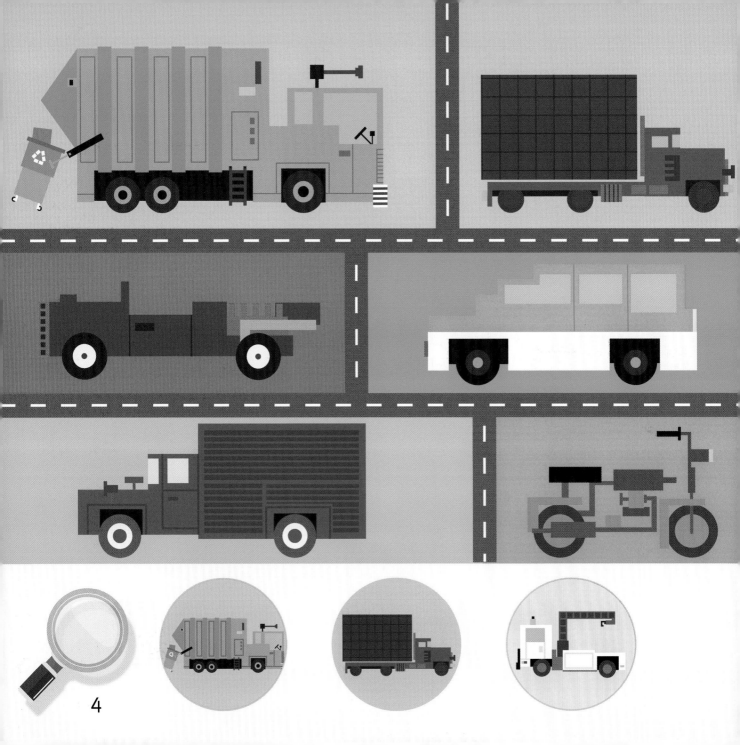

4

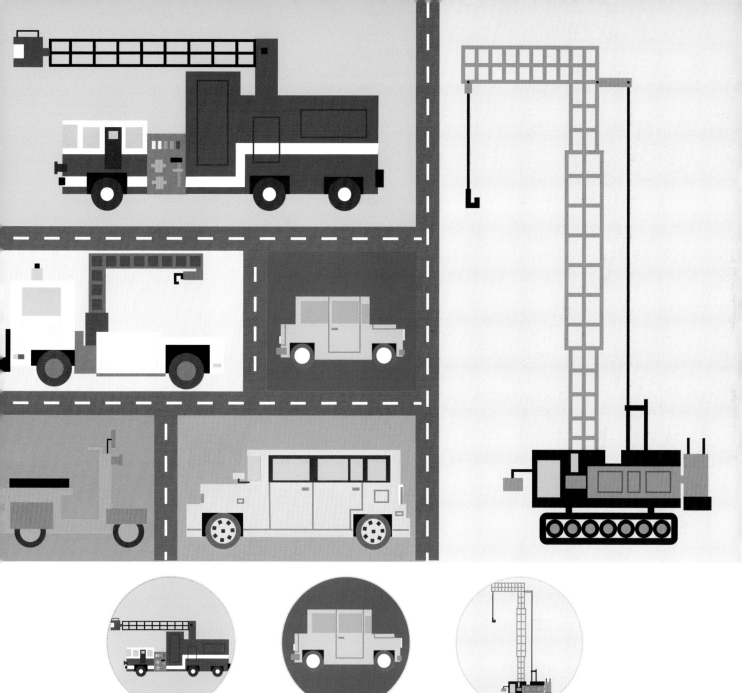

6

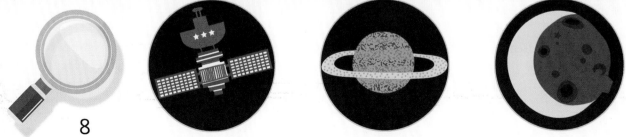

8

10

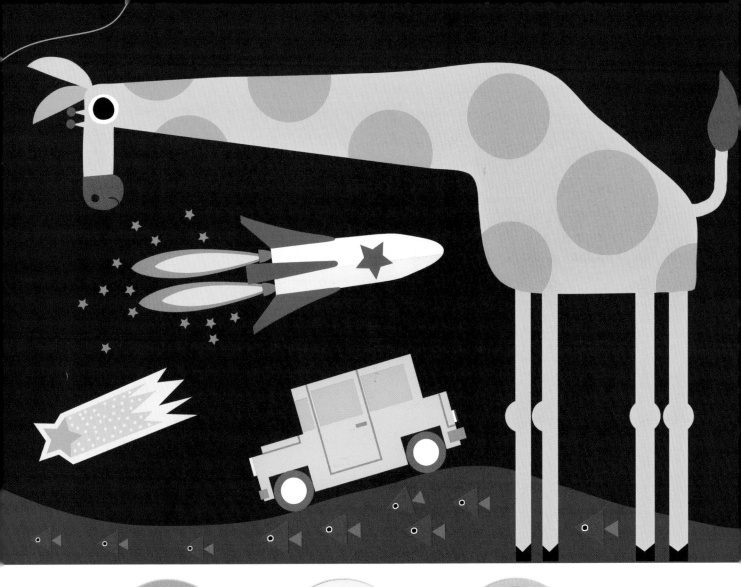

Shapes and colour

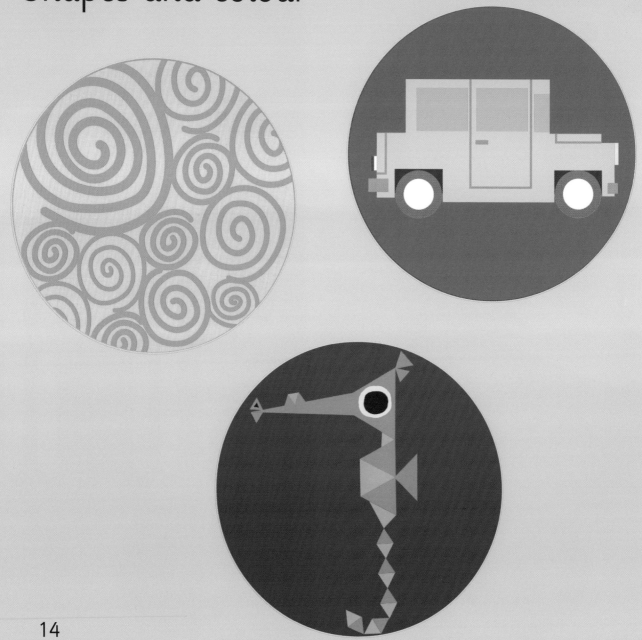

 Review: After reading

Read 1: Phonemic awareness

- Play 'find it!' by looking for the items in the small circles at the bottom of the pages, to build phonemic awareness. Choose an object or two per page and ask the children to find them in the illustration. Emphasise the initial sound of each word and then say the word. (e.g. Can you find a zzz zigzag?)
- When they have found the object, ask the children to say the first sound of the word.
- Look at pages 14 and 15 together and ask the children to describe the different shapes and colours in the pictures. Can they find any of the shapes in the book, for example: Which clothes have yellow zizags like these?

Read 2: Vocabulary

- Encourage the children to hold the book and turn the pages.
- Spend time looking at the pictures and discussing them, drawing on any relevant experience or knowledge the children have. Encourage them to talk about what they can see in each picture, giving as much detail as they can. Expand the children's vocabulary by naming objects in the illustrations that they do not know.
- Sound-talk an object or two from the circles at the bottom of each page. (e.g. Can you find the m-oo-n?) Sound-talk but do not blend the word. When the children find the object, encourage them to blend the word.

Read 3: Comprehension

- Read the book again. Ask:
  - o (on each page) What shapes can you see here? What are they on or part of?
  - o On pages 4 and 5: Which shapes make up, e.g. the lorry? What shape are the wheels?